# Social Media for Successful Film Promotion

# Table of Contents

Social media is not just an activity; it is an investment of valuable time and resources. Surround yourself with people who not just support you and stay with you, but inform your thinking about ways to WOW your online presence

# Chapter 1. Introduction

Welcome to our Special Report on arguably one of the most vibrant and exciting domains today: Social Media for Successful Film Promotion! In this rapidly shifting digital landscape, leveraging social media platforms is no longer just an option, but a necessity for the film industry. But fear not, this report is crafted to be your compass, guiding you through the whirlwind of hashtags, shares, and likes. You'll uncover how to take your film from being just another title to becoming a compelling, must-watch sensation. Reignite the magic of movies within people's hearts by mastering the techniques of social media film promotion! This thoroughly engaging and informative report is a must-read for anyone aiming to score a standing ovation in the box-office world. See you on the inside!

# Chapter 2. Unveiling the Power of Social Media

In the ever-evolving world of film marketing and promotion, the phenomenon known as social media stands tall as a formidable player. This chapter shall serve as your guided excursion into the depths of this powerful platform that has changed the game of movie promotion at its core. We will elucidate the dynamic aspects of social media, its essentiality in today's digitized world, the analysis of its audience and a detailed inspection of its transformational impact on the film industry.

## 2.1. The Blooming Landscape of Social Media

In the vast wilderness of the digital landscape, social media blooms like an ever-expansive jungle. With diverse platforms like Facebook, Instagram, Twitter, Snapchat, and TikTok, social media is a sprawling cosmos of user-generated content, where interaction, communication, and information sharing happen real-time.

It's a force majeure, an unstoppable giant. According to a report by Datareportal, as of 2021, about 4.48 billion people actively use social media, equating to about 57% of the global population! This astounding stat reflects the omnipresence of social media in our lives.

These platforms have entirely altered the way we perceive the world, connect with people, interact with brands, and consume entertainment. Consequently, they have inevitably acted as catalysts in the evolution of marketing, including film promotion.

## 2.2. Audience Analysis: The Social Media Demographic

When crafting campaigns for any marketing terrain, understanding the demographics is crucial. According to recent reports, social media consumption is highest among individuals aged between 18-34, a demographic vital to the film industry worldwide. Hence this young, digitally native audience forms the heart of the social media marketing strategy for movies, shaping their promotional actions and content structure.

Also noteworthy is the geographical spread. North America, East Asia, and Northern Europe are among the regions with the highest social media penetration, indicating the regions with the most potential for film promotion.

However, high-speed internet access and the proliferation of smartphones have made social media omnipresent even in developing nations. Consequently, films can now reach corners of the world previously seen as inaccessible; a remarkable achievement, thanks to the technological prowess of social media.

## 2.3. Revolutionizing Film Promotion: The Social Media Impact

Social media has indeed marked a significant shift in film promotion strategies. Traditional methods of film promotion like billboards, TV spots, and print ads have been overshadowed by social media campaigns due to their instantaneous reach and interaction potential.

One of the most substantial benefits is audience engagement. The interactive nature of social media creates a two-way communication path. Rather than just being mere receivers, the audience is now part of the conversation, making promotion campaigns more effective, dynamic, and impactful.

Moreover, films can now create a robust online presence before their release, building anticipation and a sense of community among potential viewers. Through teasers, interactive posts, behind-the-scenes clips and more, films can sustain a prolonged period of online buzz, translating to greater excitement for the release.

The adaptability factor is another unique feature of social media. Campaigns can swiftly modify their strategies according to the ever-changing online trends and audience responses. This empowers the promotional campaigns, offering them the ability to iterate and improve continually.

Social media also diversifies the promotional strategies by offering various modes of content. Be it a 140-character tweet, a stunning poster on Instagram, a gripping trailer on YouTube, or a playful challenge on TikTok - each platform allows films to uniquely express and promote themselves.

## 2.4. Conclusion

The evolution of social media has unlocked a world of possibilities in influencing perceptions, creating buzz, and shaping the success of a movie. The ability to reach audiences globally, interact and engage with them directly, and adapt in real-time to their feedback has reinvented film promotion strategies.

Today, it's safe to say, social media's power and reach are vital for any film promotion to make a mark in people's minds and hearts. However, the excitement lies in understanding and strategizing around these diverse platforms which bear their unique rewards. The subsequent chapters of this report will take you through this journey, enabling you to harness the power of each one to your advantage.

The advent of social media has indeed made the world a global village, transforming the way we promote movies. It's time to unravel the rest of this fascinating realm as we venture deeper into the insightful exploration of social media for film promotion.

# Chapter 3. Understanding Social Media Platforms: From Facebook to TikTok

The chapter begins with the exploration of various social media platforms, covering well-established zones like Facebook, moving onto professional platforms like LinkedIn, to visual-centric Instagram, video-sharing behemoth YouTube, creative platform Pinterest, microblogging giant Twitter, super-informal Snapchat and ending with explosive newcomer TikTok. The essence of this chapter is to provide a broad understanding of these different platforms and their uniqueness, so as to be able to create a strategic road map in promoting a film.

## 3.1. The Giants: Facebook and LinkedIn

Facebook, as of the third quarter of 2021, boasts an astronomical figure of almost 2.91 billion active users globally, rendering it a crucial player in our quest for successful film promotion. Facebook allows users to share posts, images, videos, and much more, and this universal approach makes it an ideal platform for a broad spectrum of promotional strategies. Interestingly, Facebook's algorithm continues to prioritize visually dynamic content like videos and images, making it the perfect platform for trailers, video clips, and candid shots from film sets.

While LinkedIn may be viewed primarily as a business networking and job search platform, its ability to reach a more targeted, professional demographic should not be overlooked. LinkedIn's user base is more mature than most social platforms and tends to contain decision-makers, adding to its potential for influencing pivotal crowds in film promotion. A well-crafted film synopsis or interview with the director can resonate exceptionally well here.

## 3.2. The Visual Artists: Instagram and Pinterest

Instagram, with over one billion active users monthly, has become the go-to platform for visual storytelling. Films, being primarily visual mediums, can benefit enormously from the platform's obsession with high-quality, visually stunning content. Behind-the-scenes images, movie posters, short clips, and even candid actor shots can all create significant intrigue and anticipation for a movie.

Pinterest, though less dominant, is no less important. It thrives on images, graphics, and a thumbnail-grouping format that allows users to curate content according to personal preferences. While less interactive, it can be a great space to share your film posters, scene shots, and infographic-style film sneak peeks. It's a more passive form of engagement, but branding possibilities here are abundant.

## 3.3. The Content Paradise: YouTube

In the world of social media platforms, YouTube stands as the unchallenged monarch of video content. It provides an unrivalled opportunity to reach all demographics through video sharing. From posting trailers and song releases to sharing behind-the-scenes footage and interviews with the cast and crew, YouTube is perfect for extensive, detailed content that increases anticipation and gives film enthusiasts a manageable dose of what the film intends to offer.

# 3.4. The Instant Pot: Twitter and Snapchat

Twitter, with its 280 character limit, thrives on brevity, immediacy, and discussion. While it may initially seem less suitable for film promotion, it's worth noting that Twitter is often where things trend first. Cleverly curated movie quotes, enticing one-liners about the plot, or a well-timed Tweet about a film-related event can generate substantial engagement.

Snapchat is unique in its ephemeral content approach. Content on Snapchat disappears after 24 hours and is thus ideal for real-time, casual, and engaging content. Sneak peeks, countdowns, and real-time updates from premieres are some ways to stir excitement in Snapchat's typically younger user base.

# 3.5. The Rookie Star : TikTok

TikTok has grown phenomenally in recent years. Short, viral videos are its bread and butter, creating an ideal platform for film promotions. Dance-offs, mimics, or short clips with a catchy dialogue from the film can become fast-spreading trends on TikTok. TikTok challenges and user-generated content around the film can lead to organic promotion, which often resonates more.

In conclusion, understanding the unique aspects of each social media platform enables us to design an effective film promotion strategy. By tailoring the presentation and style of content to each platform's norms and user preferences, we increase our chances of cutting through the noise and making our film a topic of conversation. Film promotion on social media isn't about spamming each platform with the same content but strategically using the unique strengths each platform possesses. Flawless execution of this understanding can be an elixir for the film – waking it from obscurity and taking it to the much coveted limelight.

# Chapter 4. Tailoring Your Message: Content Creation for Film Promotion

Valid and compelling content is the key driving force behind successful social media strategies. As such, a film's success in this digital era heavily relies on its content's relevance, attractiveness, and impact on the target audience. For films, content creation involves curating messages that effectively communicate the storyline, the characters, and the unique selling proposition that sets the film apart from others.

## 4.1. The Dynamics of Target Audience

The fundamental pillar of tailoring your message for successful film promotion is understanding the dynamics of your target audience - their preferences, interests, and social media consumption habits. This understanding is pivotal in creating content that resonates with them.

To conduct a comprehensive analysis of your audience, you must decipher their demographics, psychographics, and behavioristics. Demographics represent their age, gender, location, and income level. This analysis aids in understanding which social media platform they frequent and what type of content they likely consume. Psychographics are about their values, attitudes, and interests, integral for shaping the tone, story, and aesthetics of your content. Behavioristics, on the other hand, include their consumption habits - when and how much they engage with social media. This dictates the timing and frequency of your posts.

Once you fully comprehend your audience's dynamics, you can effectively tailor your film's content based on their preferences.

## 4.2. Crafting Unique Selling Proposition

To captivate your audience, you need to identify your film's unique selling proposition (USP) and integrate it into your content. Every film is a distinct universe, offering a unique set of characters, narrative, atmosphere, soundtrack, artistic choices, etc. The trick is to identify these unique aspects and make them stand out in your content.

Your film's USP could be its outstanding screenplay, breathtaking cinematography, stellar cast or the gripping plotline - anything distinctive that could woo your audience into watching the film. By accentuating these elements in your promotional content, you can create a compelling curiosity, an irresistible pull that drives the audience towards theater screens or digital platforms.

## 4.3. The Art and Science of Message Construction

Creating a tailored message is both art and science. It is an art as it requires creative thinking, clever storytelling, and sharp wit. It's a science because it involves data-driven decisions, result-oriented tactics, and a methodical approach.

Your promotional content should aim at emphasizing your film's USP in a powerful, appealing, and evocative manner. Whether it's a heart-wrenching dialogue, thrilling chase scene, or a sublimely picturesque shot - ensure your content promotes these parts effectively. The narration needs to create an emotional connection with the audience, inciting intrigue, excitement, sentimentality or thrill that draws viewers to your film.

A vital aspect of message construction is consistency. An inconsistent message can confuse your audience. Therefore, ensure that your promotional content across all platforms aligns with your core promotional theme and story.

# 4.4. The Balancing Act: Emotion and Information

Striking the right balance between emotion and information is crucial for your tailored content. While information about your film such as its release date, cast, director, and genre are necessary, should the content be entirely informational, it may fail to engage the audience effectively.

Emotionally charged content can foster deeper connections with your audience. By weaving emotional threads into your message, you can touch the audience's heartstrings, intensifying their eagerness to see the film. Whether it's the excitement promo for an action film, the ominous dread for a horror flick or the intense passion for a romantic drama - make sure the emotional fabric reflects in your content.

In contrast, bombarding your audience with emotional content but failing to provide essential information about the film is also ineffective. Remember, a balanced blend of emotion and information can create content that is both heart-tugging and informative.

# 4.5. A New Dawn: Socially Conscious Messaging

In this era of increasing social consciousness, content that reverberates with strong values and positive societal messages can strike a pertinent chord with the audience. If your film's storyline or theme aligns with popular social concerns - race, gender, environment or mental health, your promotional content should highlight this.

Not only would such messaging resonate with your audience's consciousness, but it also shows the film's engagement with issues that matter for them. Such socially-conscious promotional content can invite a wider reception, creating buzz not just about the film but the issue in focus as well.

In conclusion, tailoring your message for successful film promotion requires a deep understanding of your audience, clear identification of your film's USP, tactful construction of messages, balanced inclusion of emotion and information, and a receptiveness to socially conscious themes. The magic of movies lies not just in the story it tells on screen but also in the narrative it weaves on social media platforms.

# Chapter 5. Visual Storytelling: Creating Engaging Trailers for Social Media

In the grand architecture of film promotion, visual storytelling remains a structural cornerstone, a medium that communicates the film's essence, its ethos, its offer to audiences worldwide. Creating engaging trailers is an art, a delicate intermingling of capturing attention, evoking emotions, and treading the fine line between revelation and intrigue. Today, in the digital world's instant gratification-driven ethos, where screen sizes are shrinking but engagements are soaring, the importance of creating engaging trailers for social media is magnified.

## 5.1. The Role of Trailers in Film Promotion

Traditionally, trailers have served the purpose of being a sneak peek into the project, teasing the audience with glimpses of the visual spectacle to come. Over time, as consumption patters changed and audiences grew more discerning, trailers evolved. Today, trailers shoulder multiple responsibilities. To begin with, they ooze a sense of appeal. A way of gaining audience traction and generating interest, they are a film's anthem, its calling card to the world, a showreel encapsulating the essence of the film in a matter of minutes, or sometimes even seconds.

Secondly, trailers, especially on social media platforms, function as a catalyst for discussion. An intriguing trailer sparks conversations, fosters debates, and may even spawn a wealth of fan theories, all serving to keep the film in the public consciousness even before its release. In the era of the Internet, word-of-mouth has escalated to become word-on-the-screen, and a good trailer with enough hooks becomes the springboard for this buzz.

Finally, the trailer also subtly communicates the value proposition of the film. Are we here for an emotional journey, a laugh riot, epic visual effects, or simply to watch the magic of an acclaimed director unfold? The trailer, through its narrative, aspects such as dialogue snippets, visuals, sound design, and music, subtly primes the audience towards what they can expect.

# 5.2. Crafting Trailers for Social Media: A Different Ball Game

Creating trailers for social media involves a shift from traditional trailer-making formats. To start with, social media trailers must be optimized for a variety of screen sizes. From the giant screens of desktop monitors to the more pocket-friendly mobile screen, accommodating variability is inherent to social media trailer design.

Moreover, the social media attention span is notoriously short-lived, and engagement drops significantly after the first few seconds. Hence, a social media trailer needs to capture attention instantly. Starting with a bang, a shock, a laugh, or anything that commands immediate attention is a popular strategy.

Incorporating a call-to-action, like 'tag a friend,' 'share if you agree,' or 'like if you can't wait,' motivates viewer engagement and propels the spread of the trailer.

# 5.3. The Art and Science of Trailer Making

While there are no fixed rules for creating a perfect trailer, some common practices can enhance its effectiveness substantially. The first step is having a clear understanding of the target audience. For instance, an animated movie primarily for children may benefit from trailer visuals that are bright, energetic, playful and filled with lovable characters. A horror movie, on the other hand, might opt for somber colors, eerie music and plenty of suspenseful moments that provoke the 'chill down the spine.'

Structure matters in trailer construction, comprising ideally of a beginning that draws viewers in, a middle that presents snippets of the plot, and an end that offers a cliffhanger. Using music effectively is another important factor in trailers. Music sets the emotional tone for the film, hinting at the type of journey the viewer can expect.

Utilizing dialogues from the film can also contribute significantly to the trailer's allure- a profound quote, a sarcastic response, or a poignant statement can stay with the viewer and motivate them to pursue the film when it is released. Keeping the focus on the main characters and giving glimpses of their journey in the film also enhances the trailer's effectiveness.

# 5.4. Measuring the Success of A Trailer

How does one measure a trailer's success in the social media realm? Is it through views or shares, likes or comments? While these are certainly important metrics, more critical is the sentiment behind these numbers. The quantity of views or shares matters little if the audience's sentiment is negative. Hence, along with the numbers, it's imperative to assess the qualitative feedback. What are people saying in the comments, on Twitter threads, on discussion forums like Reddit?

Critically evaluating this feedback can provide crucial insights- Are people intrigued? Are they appreciative of the visuals, the music, the actor's performance? Is there excitement, or is there criticism? Being receptive to these critiques allows marketers to assess the pulse of their audience, learn what works, and more importantly, unravel what does not.

In the end, creating engaging trailers for social media is both an art and a science. It requires creativity, intuition, and empathy to tap into the emotions of the audience and analytical prowess to assess the effectiveness of these endeavors. After all, a trailer builds a bridge between the film and its audience, and in this era of social media, bridge-building has never been more crucial. The lights have dimmed, the audience is waiting, it's time to roll the trailer and let your film begin to shine!

# Chapter 6. Hashtag Heaven: Effective Hashtags and Their Role in Promotion

In the bustling arena of social media, trends come and go, but the art of using hashtags has firmly cemented its position as a vital element in successful social media promotion. Indeed, in the world of film promotion, effective hashtag usage can be the decisive factor that transforms a film from a mere cinematic feature into a viral sensation. By implementing strategic hashtag campaigns, a movie can penetrate the vast digital landscape by turning social media users into active participants, message amplifiers, and, ultimately, avid viewers. However, creating a dynamic and potent hashtag does not merely revolve around conceiving a catchy phrase. Rather, it necessitates deep understanding, creative foresight, and strategic planning. With this in mind, the following sections will provide a detailed and comprehensive exploration of the cogent role of hashtags and show how they serve as a linchpin in successful film promotion.

## 6.1. Understanding Hashtags

Hashtags, represented by the pound or hash symbol (#), are tools used to aggregate content on social media platforms. Originally used on Twitter, their utility has expanded to other platforms such as Instagram, Facebook, and LinkedIn. Whenever a user incorporates a hashtag into their post, it becomes discoverable to other users—even those who don't follow them—when they search for that specific hashtag.

Utilising hashtags equips your content with the opportunity to be discovered by a larger audience, inclusive of those who may not be initially aware of the film. By using popular, pertinent, or even bespoke hashtags, your film's promotional content can be targeted to user interest areas, thereby pulling your potential audience towards your content magnetically, regardless of the vastness of the social media sphere.

## 6.2. Crafting The Perfect Hashtag

The formation of an effective hashtag requires a blend of creativity, relevancy, and a compact representation of your film's essence. It is advisable to make it unique to your movie, something memorable yet simple. The hashtag should be in alignment with the movie's theme, plot, and overall vibe, serving as a microcosm of the movie itself. At the same time, it should stimulate curiosity, incite conversations, and encourage social media users to latch onto it and share it with their followers.

Choosing the right words is crucial. Ideally, it should be a short phrase or a clever combination of words. Be cautious to avoid any ambiguity that could lead to misinterpretation. Test the hashtag before rolling it out. Evoke thoughts, feelings, or actions linked to your film, enticing your audience to explore and engage more with your content.

## 6.3. Launching and Promoting Your Hashtag

The strategy behind launching your hashtag can be just as important as creating it. Timing is key. Introduce your hashtag when you've garnered a substantial amount of attention for your film's social media promotion—this could coincide with the release of your film's trailer or a major announcement. Ensure that your hashtag is consistently used across all your promotional posts. Encourage your film's cast, crew, and prominent influencers to use it in their posts, further enhancing its reach and visibility.

Promoting your hashtag can also involve creating compelling content around it like contests, quizzes, or interactive posts that would encourage user-generated content. User-generated content boosts the authenticity of your promotion by incorporating personal experiences of real people, rendering your promotion more relatable and engaging.

# 6.4. Evaluating Hashtag Performance

A well-executed hashtag strategy must be accompanied by evaluation and monitoring. This enables assessing the success of your campaign and gaining valuable insights for future strategies. Various tools are available to track hashtag performance across different platforms such as Instagram Insights, TweetReach, and Keyhole. These tools can provide valuable metrics such as total impressions, reach, engagement, top posts, and crucially, content generated by your audience using your hashtag.

Keep a vigilant eye on your hashtag's performance, assess the engagement, and do not shy away from tweaking your strategy, if essential. Experience is the best teacher in the happening world of social media. There is always room for improving your game.

In conclusion, mastering hashtags is not about exploiting a trendy tool, but about understanding and embracing it as an efficient method of communicating with your audience. A well-crafted hashtag, as part of a well-orchestrated promotional stratagem, can most certainly turn your film into a successful saga in the web space.

# Chapter 7. Mind the Trend: Leveraging Viral Challenges and Memes in Film Promotion

The advent of the internet and the pervasiveness of social media platforms have revolutionized the ways in which we access, consume, and share content daily. One of the most interesting aspects of this shift is how it has turned cultural phenomena such as viral challenges and internet memes into powerful promotional tools for various industries, including film. When harnessed effectively, these aspects can generate buzz, cultivate online communities, and enhance the visibility of films in a global digital landscape crowded with content vying for attention.

## 7.1. Viral Challenges: Fueling Engagement through Participation

In recent years, viral challenges have taken the social media world by storm. These are typically fun, interactive, and user-generated content that call for people to participate and share their performances online, often under a specific hashtag. They range from lighthearted to thought-provoking, physical to creative. The critical factor that makes viral challenges effective promotional tools is their ability to fuel audience engagement and participation.

For film promotion, these challenges often align with the theme, plot, or characters of the movie, adding an immersive, participatory dimension to traditional marketing methods. For instance, using a dance sequence from your film and converting that into a challenge, like the #InMyFeelingsChallenge for Drake, encourages viewers to actively engage with your content. As participants share their iterations and responses, the challenge spreads, effectively creating a ripple effect. This user-generated content not only raises visibility for the film but also creates an interactive experience that can heighten the anticipation and excitement surrounding its release.

Successful implementation of a viral challenge for film promotion demands meticulous planning and execution. It involves studying the social media landscape, understanding what types of challenges resonate with your target audience, crafting a challenge that aligns with the film's content, and deploying it at the right time to capture maximum attention.

# 7.2. Memes: Tapping into Viral Humor and Culture

Memes, humorous images or videos that are copied and spread rapidly by internet users, have become a language unto themselves in the digital age. The amusing nature of memes and their ability to quickly spread across social media platforms make them an excellent tool for film promotion.

In Hollywood, the movie promotion strategists have started extensively utilizing the meme culture, noting its ability to reach vast audiences with minimal investment. Indeed, the beauty of memes lies in their ability to capture the essence of a message succinctly and humorously, eliciting emotional responses that can enhance recall and association. A cleverly crafted meme can encapsulate the spirit, dialogue, or quirk of a character, or a pivotal moment in a film, stirring curiosity and making audiences want to explore more.

For example, the "Distracted Boyfriend" meme was repurposed for promoting the film "Zombieland: Double Tap," featuring the primary characters in a humorous context. This tactic not only entertained audiences but also sparked conversations about the film, helping maintain its relevance leading up to the release.

Creating an effective meme for film promotion, however, requires an understanding of meme culture and catching onto trends. It's a delicate balance of humor, cultural relevance, and strategically embedded promotional content. Moreover, an understanding of different social media platforms can help you tailor memes to the specificities of different platforms for optimal reach and engagement.

# 7.3. Conclusion: The Power of Trends in Film Promotion

Riding the wave of viral challenges and memes requires creativity, a deep understanding of digital culture, and efficient social media management. However, when successful, these strategies can translate into higher audience engagement, stronger online presence, and ultimately, robust ticket sales.

The innovative world of viral challenges and memes awaits. By embracing these strategies, you can create a promotional campaign that resonates with today's social media-savvy audiences, captivating their attention and leaving a lasting impression, thereby translating into a successful film promotion. Remember, in our interconnected digital age, your movie is not just competing with other movies; it's competing for the attention and engagement of audiences who are constantly bombarded with content. Use this challenge as an opportunity to think outside the traditional promotional box and ply the seas of viral social media trends - your ticket to box-office success could be just one viral challenge or meme away.

# Chapter 8. Influencer Culture: Harnessing the Stardom for Your Film

Influencer culture stands as a vital pillar in crafting a successful film promotion strategy in the current digital age. As we navigate this chapter, we'll delve into the world of influencers, understand their reach and role in film promotion, and how to effectively harness their stardom for your project's success.

## 8.1. The Emergence of Influencer Culture

The advent of social media has birthed a new type of celebrity: the influencer. Unlike traditional celebrities who usually earned their fame through film, music or sports, influencers build their followership through creating engaging content on various social media platforms. This path to stardom thrives on personal interaction, authenticity, and digital savviness. Influencers are seen as everyday people who, through their unique perspectives and dynamic content, amass followers who value their opinions and recommendations. This implies that leveraging the right influencers can heighten the buzz around a movie, thereby attracting a larger audience and accumulating massive returns.

## 8.2. Understanding Influencer Tiers

To harness the power of influencers, first, it's crucial to understand the different tiers of influencers. Each tier has a unique reach, engagement level, and influence, making them suitable for different promotional objectives:

1. Micro-Influencers: These are influencers with about 1,000 to 50,000 followers. They typically enjoy high engagement levels due to their close-knit community. Tapping into this group is ideal for reaching a niche audience with a strong, personalized message.

2. Mid-Tier Influencers: They have between about 50,000 to 500,000 followers. They offer a balance between reach and engagement, making them an excellent option for broader messaging that still needs a personalized touch.

3. Macro-Influencers: These include influencers with 500,000 to a million followers. With a larger reach, they are ideal for widespread message dissemination but may not have the same engagement levels as lower tiers.

4. Mega-Influencers: They possess over one million followers. Their vast reach might compromise personal engagement but is highly valuable for mass awareness campaigns.

# 8.3. Influencer Selection for Film Promotion

Selecting influencers for film promotion is a strategic process that entails a blend of art and science. Here are steps to guide you:

1. Define your Audience: Who is your movie catered towards? What is their demographic profile? What platforms do they spend most of their time on?

2. Identify Influencers Resonating with Your Audience: Research the type of content your target audience engages with. Which influencers do they follow? Which ones align with the values and theme of your movie?

3. Evaluate Influencer Metrics: Beyond follower count, assess engagement rates, previous partnership successes, and audience sentiment.

## 8.4. The Power of Authentic Connection

Influencers are successful because they cultivate an authentic connection with their followers. When an influencer promotes a movie, the message is more readily received as it is perceived as a recommendation from a trusted friend. Therefore, ensuring alignment between your film's messaging and the influencer's persona and brand is highly critical.

## 8.5. Activating Influencers in your Film Promotion Campaign

Having selected your influencers, you need to determine how they will fit into your promotion plan. This could involve sponsored posts, engaging the influencers with the film (such as special screenings or exclusive set visits), having them share exclusive content (behind-the-scenes clips or interviews with cast members), or even creative routes like involving them in the movie itself.

## 8.6. Managing Influencer Relationships

Building and maintaining strong relationships with influencers is equally as important to utilize their star power. Open lines of communication, fair compensation, respect for their creative autonomy, and reasonable expectations are key to fostering these relationships.

# 8.7. Evaluating the Impact of Influencer Marketing

To measure the success of your strategy, monitor key metrics such as engagement on influencer posts, referral traffic to your official pages, and conversions to ticket sales or streaming views.

In conclusion, influencer culture presents a fascinating and effective avenue for propelling your film into the limelight. By strategically selecting, activating, and managing influencers, you can create a promotional campaign that strongly resonates with your target audience, igniting anticipation and driving ticket sales or streams. However, tapping into influencer culture requires understanding its intricacies and nuances. As you venture forward, remember that authenticity and strategic alignment are your guiding lights in this fascinating world of digital stardom.

# Chapter 9. Online Premieres: The New Norm in Film Launch

In an era of rapid digital transformation and advances in streaming technology, movie premieres have undergone an evolutionary transformation of their own, morphing from exclusively grand physical events to increasingly prominent online affairs. These Digital Premieres, encompassing anything from a streamed debut on a platform like Netflix or a debut live event on Twitter or Facebook, signify a colossal shift in the traditional norms of the film industry.

## 9.1. The Ascend of Online Premieres

The ascend of online premieres, much like many digital adjustments traversing the business landscape, can be attributed to the enhanced accessibility and connectivity that characterizes the digital era. We are living in the age of the internet, and technology and access to high-speed internet have enhanced how we consume content. The traditional constraints in terms of location and time have been largely disintegrated, enabling a truly global film debut.

Simultaneously, consumer evolution has also played a key role. The modern movie-goer is digitally savvy, convenience-driven, and comfortable with consuming content on digital platforms. As such, viewer habits and preferences have tremendously influenced the advent and acceptance of online premieres.

## 9.2. Maneuvering the Digital Stage

Online movie premieres are exhilarating yet complex to navigate. A successful online premiere requires extensive planning, robust technology, and a deep understanding of the digital landscape. Following are some key considerations:

1) Platform Choice: The platform for your online premiere serves as your movie theater. Therefore, choosing the right platform, where you can reach your target demographic and which provides a seamless streaming experience, is critical. Whether it's a dedicated streaming site like Netflix, Hulu, or Amazon Prime, or a social media site like Facebook, YouTube, or Twitter depends on your film and its intended audience.

2) Audience Notification: Ensure your intended viewers are aware of the online premiere. Utilize your film's social media channels, email marketing, digital press releases, interviews, and more to spread the word.

3) Technical Aspects: The quality of the streaming experience is of utmost importance. Ensure to test all technical aspects beforehand and have a team on standby to handle any unexpected issues.

4) Engagement: Unlike physical premieres, online premieres can sometimes lack the immediate audience engagement and feedback. To address this, consider adding engaging elements such as live chat, Q&As, or comment sections to boost interaction.

# 9.3. Social Media for Online Premieres

Social media, as an innate online platform, complements online premieres by allowing films to cast a wider net and reach audiences globally. By organically stirring conversation around the film, generating buzz, and fostering a community of fans, social media plays a key role in successfully executing an online launch.

Through posts sharing behind-the-scenes content, film teasers, cast interviews, and fan engagement activities, social media holds immense potential to pique interest and build momentum leading up to the premiere. Moreover, during the premiere, features like Watch Party on Facebook and Twitter's live feature can encourage synchronous viewing amongst fans, mimicking an authentic theater experience in the online space.

# 9.4. The Future of Premieres

In an increasingly connected world, the trend of online premieres is only likely to amplify in the future. As films explore this new frontier, industry stakeholders must adapt their promotional strategies. Social media plays an instrumental role in leveraging online premieres for successful film promotion, and exploring its potential could well be the holy grail of next-generation film marketing.

In conclusion, the transition to online premieres is a testament to how technology, consumer behavior, and social media are crafting the future of film launches. By acknowledging this shifting paradigm and leveraging the tools within reach, filmmakers can maximize their launch success in the digital domain. Nevertheless, the essence remains: creating compelling stories that resonate with audiences. As the landscape evolves, so must the approach to narrating these stories, promising a thrilling journey further in the realm of cinema.

# Chapter 10. Evaluating Success: Metrics That Matter in Social Media Promotion

It's an exhilarating moment when you finally launch your promotional campaign into the digital universe. Every click, like, share, and comment is met with mounting anticipation, but these seemingly important interactions are just the surface of what makes a campaign successful. To truly evaluate the efficiency and success of your film promotional efforts, you need to harness the power of analytics, and that means understanding the Key Performance Indicators (KPIs) that really matter on social media.

## 10.1. Unraveling the Mystery of KPIs

KPIs, or Key Performance Indicators, are quantifiable metrics that demonstrate how effectively a campaign is achieving its objectives. There are many KPIs at your disposal, so the first step is to understand which ones align most closely with your goals. Essentially, different KPIs hold different importance depending upon your objectives. For example, if your goal is to maximize brand awareness, then the number of shares or the reach of your campaign might be a crucial KPI for you. On the other hand, if you're aiming to boost movie sales, then conversion rates will most likely take center stage.

## 10.2. The Different Types of Social Media Metrics

Exhaustive social media analytics can be categorized broadly under four major heads - reach, engagement, conversions, and consumer sentiment.

1. Reach: This refers to the total number of users who have come across your movie promotion on their social media feeds. It's a top-funnel metric and lays the groundwork for other key metrics, giving you an idea of how widespread your campaign is.

2. Engagement: This involves all the interactions users have with your promotional content such as likes, comments, shares, clicks, and even video views. High engagement generally signifies that your content resonates with your audience.

3. Conversions: More aligned to the bottom-funnel outcomes, conversion metrics monitor actions that have direct business outcomes, such as ticket sales or subscriptions generated from your social media posts. Tracking the source of these conversions helps in allocating budgets effectively for future campaigns.

4. Consumer Sentiment: This gauge of public opinion about your film provides a qualitative element to your metrics, indicating not just what people do in relation to your content, but what they think and feel about it.

# 10.3. Crunching the Numbers: Detailed Guide to Key Metrics

Once outlined broad categories, let's delve into the specific metrics, understanding their relevance to your campaign.

1. Impressions and Reach: Impressions refers to the number of times your content was shown, regardless of being clicked or not. On the other hand, reach denotes the number of unique users who saw your post. A wide disparity between impressions and reach could signify that your content is being viewed multiple times by the same users. If your reach is low, it might be time to broaden your targeting.

2. Click-Through Rate (CTR): This metric tells you how many users clicked on your sponsored post, trailer, or call to action. A low CTR may mean your content is not compelling enough, or it's not reaching the right audience.

3. Shares and Comments: Unlike likes, shares and comments indicate a higher level of user engagement. If your posts are sparking conversations and being shared, it likely means you've struck a chord with your audience.

4. Conversion Rate: This tells you how many visitors completed a desired action, such as purchasing a ticket, subscribing to a newsletter, or claiming a discount. If it's low, there's a mismatch somewhere between your promotional content and the target audience.

5. Sentiment Analysis: This metric provides insight into the tone and context of the conversations about your film and campaign. Rather than just analyzing numbers, it helps to capture and quantify those innumerable feelings and thoughts shared by the audience on social media platforms.

# 10.4. Using Tools to Monitor Your Metrics

Effectively analyzing these metrics requires specific tools and software. These range from built-in analytics like Facebook Insights or YouTube Analytics, to third-party applications like Hootsuite, Buffer, or Sprout Social. The beauty of these tools lies not just in their ability to capture and quantify data, but their power to translate numbers into meaningful, actionable insights.

# 10.5. An Ongoing Process: Continual Analysis and Course Correction

It's essential to understand that evaluating the success of your campaign isn't an event, but an ongoing process. Constantly monitoring your metrics and comparing them with your goals allows for data-driven adjustments that keep your campaign on track. This dynamic process of analysis and course correction ultimately leads you closer to success.

Evaluating digital metrics can seem like you're adrift in a sea of data, but once you grasp the key metrics and tools, each data point acts as a lighthouse guiding your campaign to its objectives. Remember, the importance of a metric depends entirely on your promotional goals. Just like a film itself, its promotion should not just be a numbers game, it should also touch the hearts of its audience. In the ever-intriguing world of social media promotions, remember to strike a balance between data-driven decisions and the irreplaceable magic of cinema.

# Chapter 11. Case Study Analysis: Successful Social Media Campaigns for Film Promotion

Social media campaigns for film promotion highlight how various tactics and strategies, referencing from brief spiels to long narratives, from static images to dynamic movement, can catalyze a film's metrics of success, not just in the box-office receipts, but also in terms of its social presence and relevance online. This chapter will intricately dissect various case studies, perusing each detail to extract the key elements for successful film promotions.

## 11.1. The Blair Witch Project: The Pioneer

Recognized as the trailblazer in online film marketing, 'The Blair Witch Project' exploited the nascent Internet in 1999 to create a low-budget campaign that eschewed the traditional trailer or poster format. The creators designed an intriguing website that showcased fragments of the alleged myth and mystery of the Blair Witch, stirring curiosity in a way that conventional trailers could not. The audience was made to believe that what they watched was indeed real, courtesy of cleverly constructed pseudo-documentary styled narratives.

Such evocative storytelling, combined with the mystery, immediately captivated the audience's attention. Word spread like wildfire, leading up to the film's release and creating a massive drive of audience to the theatres. With just a $60,000 marketing budget, the film went on to gross over $248 million worldwide.

## 11.2. Deadpool: Pushing the Boundaries of Conventional Wisdom

2016's 'Deadpool' astounded us all with its audacious yet successful social media campaign that was anything but conventional. A combination of the anti-hero's characteristic irreverence, slapstick humor and an meticulously planned campaign turned Deadpool into an enormous success story. Through subversive and interactive marketing volleys, the Deadpool campaign mastered the art of following the narrative theme consistently across different platforms.

The campaign featured 'poop emoji' billboards, humorous Valentine's Day romantic spoofs, Deadpool's satirical advice column, and a mock Public service announcement on testicular cancer. It remained unflinchingly faithful to its central character's sensibilities, transforming Ryan Reynolds from the star of the film to an influencer who embodied the attributes and irreverence of Deadpool himself.

## 11.3. Paranormal Activity: Harnessing User-Generated Content

With a frugal budget and a highly innovative social media strategy, 'Paranormal Activity' in 2009 became one of the most profitable films in the history of cinema. On a minuscule budget of $15,000, the film utilized a 'Demand it' service via Eventful, encouraging movie-goers to request the film in their city. This helped create grassroots support and made the viewers part of the film's distribution story.

Further, they leveraged the intense reactions people had to viewing the movie by sharing the raw footage of these reactions on social media. The shared fear and terror propagated the idea of Paranormal

Activity being a "must-watch" edge-of-the-seat experience.

# 11.4. The Hunger Games Campaign: Encapsulating Immersive Experiences

The Hunger Games franchise took social media promotion to another level by creating a detailed and expansive universe online that mirrored the dystopian world in the books and films. The producers built elaborate websites for the fictional Capitol City and used Tumblr to share fashion of the Capitol, Pinterest for recipes inspired by the series, and Facebook for integrating character profiles.

The campaign also included an interactive, online game using Google maps, where users could fight their way to the Capitol. This strategy of creating an entire immersive, interactive experience out of film promotion, ensured an extensive fan following and robust box-office success for the franchise.

# 11.5. Key Takeaways

Successful film promotion through social media primarily revolves around creativity, strategic foresight, and a deep understanding of prospective audiences. Effective campaigns provide immersive experiences, narrate engaging stories, emphasize the strong points of the film, stimulate viral discussions, and often push the boundaries of conventional film promotion. And most importantly, they remain consistent with the film's core narrative and brand.

It's essential to remember that while these case studies are monumental, they represent just one facet of the intricately woven tapestry of film marketing. Each campaign requires a unique approach, tailored to its specific content, and benefiting from its individual strengths while negotiating its challenges.

Experimentation and unorthodox approach might just be the unique selling points that thrust your film into the limelight. Remember, the world of social media film promotion is as expansive as it is exciting. Skies are the limit, and beyond!

www.ingramcontent.com/pod-product-compliance
Lightning Source LLC
Chambersburg PA
CBHW071048260726
48661CB00007B/3215